CONTENTS

A Desert Food Web

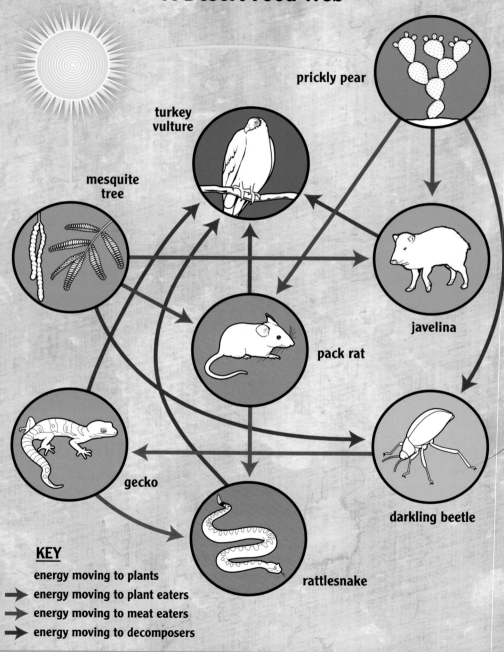

prickly pear

turkey vulture

mesquite tree

javelina

pack rat

gecko

darkling beetle

rattlesnake

4

DESERT
FOOD WEBS

BY PAUL FLEISHER

LERNER B   APOLIS

The photographs in this book are used with the permission of: © Rich Reid/National Geographic/Getty Images, backgrounds on pp 1, 6, 13, 22, 27, 33, 38, 44, 45, 46, 47; © Arthur Morris/Visuals Unlimited, p 5; © CORBIS, p 6; © John Cancalosi/Peter Arnold, Inc., pp 7, 12, 29; © Eric and David Hosking/CORBIS, p 9; © Richard Ashley/Visuals Unlimited, p 10; © Stuart Ingram/Istock.com, p 11; © PhotoDisc/Getty Images, pp 13, 19; © Hal Beral/Visuals Unlimited, p 15; © Doug Sokell/Visuals Unlimited, pp 16, 18; © Istock.com p 17; © Tom Bean, p 20; © D Steele/Photo Access/Getty Images, p 21; © age fotostock/SuperStock, pp 22, 27, 43; © Perennou Nuridsany/Photo Researchers, Inc., p 23; © Craig K. Lorenz/Photo Researchers, Inc., p 24; © John and Barbara Gerlach/Visuals Unlimited, p 25; © Gerald C. Kelley/Photo Researchers, Inc., p 26; © Joe McDonald/CORBIS, p 28; © Carlyn Galati/Visuals Unlimited, p 30; © E. R. Degginger/Photo Researchers, Inc., p 31; © Link/Visuals Unlimited, p 32; © Andrew Brown; Ecoscene/CORBIS, p 33; © Ted Wood/Aurora/Getty Images, p 34; © Ken Lucas/Visuals Unlimited, p 35; © Mike Lane/Alamy, p 36; © Darrell Gulin/CORBIS, p 37; © Lisa Limer/Stone+/Getty Images, p 38; © Ed Parker/Easi-Images/CFWImages.com, p 39; © Dr Marli Miller/Visuals Unlimited, p 40; © A.A.M. Van der Heyden/Independent Picture Service, p 41; U.S. Fish and Wildlife Service, pp 42, 47, 48; © George Grall/National Geographic/Getty Images, p. 46. Illustrations on pp 4, 14 by Zeke Smith, © Lerner Publishing Group, Inc.; map on p 8 © Laura Westlund/Independent Picture Service.

Cover: © John and Barbara Gerlach/Visuals Unlimited (top); US Fish and Wildlife Service (bottom left); © Joel Sartore/National Geographic/Getty Images (bottom right); © Rich Reid/National Geographic/Getty Images (background).

Early Bird Food Webs series diagrams created by Zeke Smith.

First published in the United Kingdom in 2008 by
Lerner Books,
Dalton House,
60 Windsor Avenue,
London SW19 2RR

Website address: www.lernerbooks.co.uk

This edition was updated and edited for UK publication by Discovery Books Ltd., Unit 3, 37 Watling Street, Leintwardine, Shropshire SY7 0LW

British Library Cataloguing in Publication Data

Fleisher, Paul
Desert food webs. - (Early bird food chains)
1. Arid regions ecology - Juvenile literature 2. Food chains (Ecology) - Juvenile literature
I. Title
577.5'4

ISBN-13: 978 1 58013 468 2

Printed in China

BE A WORD DETECTIVE

Can you find these words as you read about desert food webs? Be a detective and try to work out what they mean. You can turn to the glossary on page 46 for help.

bacteria	decomposers	lichens
cactuses	environment	nutrients
carnivores	food chain	omnivores
consumers	food web	photosynthesis
decay	herbivores	producers

This desert in Australia is sandy, hot and dry. What are other deserts like?

CHAPTER 1
DESERTS

Desert lands are very dry. The ground is rocky and dusty. Some deserts are flat. Other deserts have hills or mountains.

Deserts do not get much rain. Desert creatures must live with very little water.

Even though the desert is dry, many plants and animals live there. Cactuses thrive in the desert. Some small trees live there too. Grasses and flowers also grow in the desert.

Snakes and lizards live in the desert. So do rabbits. Mice scurry among the stones. Gazelle and mountain lions also live there.

A rattlesnake hides in some cactuses.

The desert is an important environment. An environment is the place where any creature lives. The environment includes the air, soil and weather. It also includes other plants and animals.

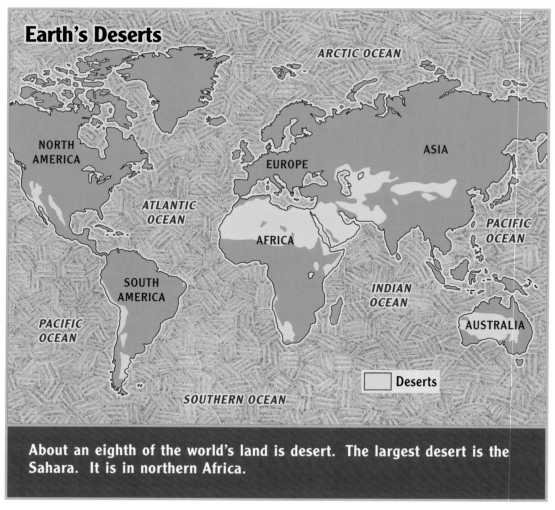

Earth's Deserts

ARCTIC OCEAN

NORTH AMERICA

EUROPE

ASIA

ATLANTIC OCEAN

AFRICA

PACIFIC OCEAN

SOUTH AMERICA

INDIAN OCEAN

PACIFIC OCEAN

AUSTRALIA

SOUTHERN OCEAN

☐ Deserts

About an eighth of the world's land is desert. The largest desert is the Sahara. It is in northern Africa.

The saguaro cactus in the middle of this picture is dead. It is breaking down. It will become part of the desert soil.

Plants and animals in the desert depend on one another. Some animals eat plants. Other animals are meat eaters. Some creatures feed on plants and animals that have died. When plants and animals die, they break down into chemicals. The chemicals become part of the soil. Some of the chemicals help plants grow. The lives of desert plants and animals are linked together.

Energy moves from one living thing to another. Living things get energy from food. A food chain shows how the energy moves. Each food chain begins with sunlight. Plants store the sun's energy. They store it as food in their roots and leaves. Animals eat the plants. They get some of the sun's energy from the plants. When one creature eats another, the energy moves along the food chain.

A bee crawls on a cactus flower. It drinks nectar from the flower. The bee gets some of the cactus's energy from the nectar.

An African gerbil gets energy by eating plant seeds. Small rodents are food for many large desert animals.

A desert has many food chains. Here is one example. Plants use the sun's energy to make seeds. A gerbil eats the seeds. Some energy goes from the plant to the gerbil. Then a owl eats the gerbil. Energy passes from the gerbil to the owl. When the owl dies, young flies and beetles eat its body. They get energy from the owl.

A food web is made of many food chains. Rats eat many kinds of seeds. They also eat fruit, roots and even insects. Hawks eat rodents, snakes and other small animals. Flies and beetles eat many different dead animals. All the foods the animals eat are part of a food web. A food web shows how all creatures in an environment depend on one another for food.

This hawk is feeding its babies meat from a small animal. Hawks get energy by eating other animals.

A desert's energy comes from the sun. Desert plants use sunlight to make food. What else do plants make?

CHAPTER 2
DESERT PLANTS

Green plants use sunlight to make food. Living things that make their own food are called producers. Animals use the food plants produce. Plants also make oxygen. Oxygen is a gas in the air. All animals need oxygen to breathe.

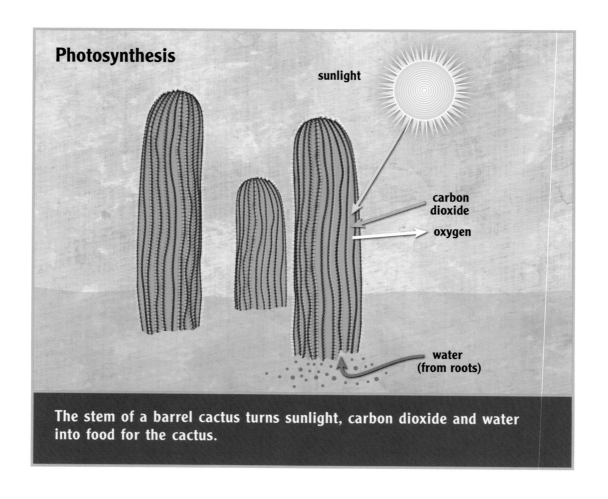

Photosynthesis

sunlight

carbon dioxide

oxygen

water (from roots)

The stem of a barrel cactus turns sunlight, carbon dioxide and water into food for the cactus.

Plants make food and oxygen through photosynthesis. Plants need sunlight and water for photosynthesis. They also need carbon dioxide. Carbon dioxide is a gas in the air. Plants take in carbon dioxide and sunlight. Their roots take in water.

Using the sun's energy, plants turn water and carbon dioxide into sugar and starch. Sugar and starch are the plants' food. Plants store the food in their leaves, stems and roots. As plants make food, they also make oxygen. The oxygen goes into the air. Animals breathe the oxygen. They breathe out carbon dioxide. Plants use the carbon dioxide to make more food.

Plants make oxygen that animals breathe. This desert animal is a chuckwalla.

Plants grow in soil. The soil contains chemicals called nutrients. Living things need nutrients to grow. Water soaks into the soil. Nutrients from the soil go into the water. The plants' roots take in the water and get nutrients from the soil. The nutrients become part of each plant.

A paloverde tree shades the ground beneath it. This keeps the soil from drying out in the hot sun.

Palm trees grow around an oasis in northern Africa. An oasis is a place in the desert that has water.

Plants need water. Desert plants cannot grow close together. There is not enough water to share. So the desert has a lot of bare ground.

Creosote bushes, growing in American deserts, do not share water. Their roots make a special chemical. The chemical keeps other plants away. The creosote bushes get all the water in the soil.

Leaves use lots of water. So desert trees lose their leaves when it gets too dry. Without leaves, they can live with very little water. Paloverde trees have green bark. When they lose their leaves, their bark makes food.

Mesquite trees grow in the desert. Their roots reach deep into the ground to get water.

The seeds of a mesquite tree are food for many desert animals.

Yellow flowers bloom on a cactus. The flowers attract birds and insects. The cactus's spines warn other hungry animals to stay away.

Cactuses grow in some deserts. Cactuses do not have leaves. They have sharp spines instead. Cactuses make food with their skin. Their thick skin holds in water. That lets them grow even when it is very dry. Cactuses live for many years. A saguaro cactus can live to be more than 100 years old.

Some desert plants live for only a short time. Their seeds wait in the ground. When it rains, the seeds grow. The new plants grow quickly. They bloom, and the desert becomes a beautiful garden. Bees and butterflies visit the flowers. The flowers make new seeds. Then the plants die. The new seeds wait in the soil. They wait for the next rainfall.

Desert wildflowers bloom after a spring rainfall.

Colourful lichens grow on rocks. Lichens are plant-like living things.

Daisies, poppies and sunflowers grow after it rains. Grasses also grow after a rainfall.

Lichens grow on desert rocks. Lichens are fungi and algae growing together. At night, dew forms on the rocks. Lichens get most of their water from dew.

A desert tortoise eats the fruit of a prickly pear cactus. What other desert animals eat plants?

CHAPTER 3
DESERT PLANT EATERS

Living things that eat other living things are consumers. *Consume* means 'eat'. Animals are consumers.

Animals that eat plants are called herbivores. The sun's energy is stored in plants. When animals eat plants, they get the sun's energy

Some desert herbivores are small. Harvester ants gather seeds to eat. They carry the seeds back to their nest. They store the seeds in the ground. Some of the seeds grow when it rains. Caterpillars eat leaves. Later, the caterpillars become butterflies. The butterflies drink from desert flowers.

A harvester ant carries a thistle seed.

Some birds are herbivores. Hummingbirds sip nectar from desert flowers. Quails scratch the soil to dig up seeds. Finches and sparrows eat seeds too.

A quail looks for food in the desert. Quails eat seeds, fruits or berries that fall to the ground.

A desert hare stands on its backlegs to reach the leaves of a desert plant.

Small and large mammals also eat plants. Gerbils are small mammals. Gerbils eat seeds and grasses. They store food in their burrows. Desert hares nibble on the leaves of desert plants. Gazelles chew on the leaves and branches of trees. They also eat grasses.

Javelinas look like pigs. They eat the juicy
stems of prickly pear cactuses. They eat cactus
fruit and seeds from trees. Javelinas also dig
up roots to eat.

A javelina uses its long teeth to bite into the pad of a prickly pear
cactus. Javelinas are also known as collared peccaries.

Meerkats hunt for other animals to eat. What are animals that eat meat called?

CHAPTER 4
DESERT MEAT EATERS

Some desert creatures eat meat. These animals are called carnivores. They catch and eat other animals. Carnivores also depend on plants. Carnivores get energy by eating animals that have eaten plants.

Spiders are carnivores. Some spiders trap insects in their webs. Tarantulas hide in burrows. They catch insects to eat. Many ants are carnivores. They eat insects and other small animals. Scorpions also hunt small animals for food.

A scorpion can snap up insects, spiders and centipedes in its large pincers. It can also sting other animals with the tip of its tail.

Roadrunners are fast runners. This roadrunner was quick enough to catch a small rattlesnake.

Many desert birds eat other animals. Woodpeckers peck cactuses to reach insects living inside. Roadrunners hunt lizards, mice and snakes. Hawks and eagles soar high in the sky. They look for small animals. These birds catch animals in their sharp claws.

Most deserts get very hot. During the day, many animals hide in the shade. It is cooler at night. Then snakes and lizards come out to hunt. The banded gecko is a lizard. It hunts at night. It hunts insects to eat. Rattlesnakes catch mice and other small mammals.

A rattlesnake swallows a small mammal.

Mountain lions are a kind of large cat. People also call them cougars or pumas. This mountain lion has caught a squirrel.

Mountain lions are some of the largest carnivores in the desert. They pounce on javelinas. They hunt for deer.

Some desert animals eat both plants and animals. These animals are called omnivores. Omnivores eat many different things. Coyotes are omnivores. They hunt small mammals and lizards. Coyotes also eat birds and eggs. They even eat fruit.

A coyote searches for desert plants and animals to eat. Coyotes eat whatever they can find.

This is a dead cactus. It is slowly breaking down. What helps it break down?

CHAPTER 5
DESERT DECOMPOSERS

When plants and animals in the desert die, they decay. They break down into nutrients. Living things called decomposers help dead things decay. Decomposers feed on dead plants and animals.

Decomposers are nature's recyclers. They help break down dead plants and animals. Nutrients in the dead plants and animals go back into the soil. Then other living things can use the nutrients. Without decomposers, the desert would be full of dead things. Then no new plants could grow and animals would run out of food.

A dead camel decays in a desert. Tiny decomposers turn its body into nutrients. Plants use the nutrients to grow.

Darkling beetles eat dead plants. They also eat dead insects.

Many insects feed on dead things. Ants often eat dead animals and so do flies and beetles.

Some insects eat dead plants. When a cactus dies, insects feed on it. The soft parts of the cactus decay. When a tree dies, termites eat the wood. They slowly turn the wood into soil.

Birds can help break down dead things. Vultures fly over the desert. They search for dead animals to eat.

A vulture stands on a dead animal. Vultures can see and smell dead animals from very far away.

Fungi grow on plants, such as this dead cactus. Bacteria also grow on the cactus.

Fungi and bacteria feed on dead plants and animals. Bacteria are much too small to see, but they are very important decomposers. Bacteria and fungi work slowly in the desert. That is because the desert is dry. Bacteria and fungi grow best when it is damp. So dead things rot very slowly in the desert.

People build villages, towns and cities in the desert. What can happen when a desert city gets too big?

CHAPTER 6
PEOPLE AND DESERTS

People have lived in deserts around the world for thousands of years. People have also built towns and cities in the desert. Big cities use lots of water and the desert does not have much

These people live in the desert in Namibia, Africa. They are the native people of the desert and they have lived there for hundreds of years.

People even farm in the desert. Farmers grow fruits and vegetables. Crops do well in the warm sunshine, but the farmers have to water their fields. They have to use lots of water so the crops do not dry up.

Rivers carry water through the desert. People get water from the rivers. People dig deep wells to find water underground. Many people want to live and farm in the desert, but the desert does not have enough water for everyone.

A river flows through the desert. Many desert streams and rivers appear only after it rains. Then they dry up again.

An ocotillo is a good plant for desert gardens. It doesn't need much water.

People in the desert must use water carefully. They must save water when they bathe and wash. They should grow plants that do not need too much water. People should grow plants that do not need too much water.

Some people people drive cars on desert lands. This damages the lands and the plants. It takes a long time for the plants to grow back.

Some desert lands have been turned into parks. No one can build homes or hunt in the parks. People cannot drive over the land. Plants and animals in desert parks are kept safe.

This fence surrounds land where desert tortoises live. The fence keeps out people and other animals.

A Harris hawk perches on a saguaro cactus.

Deserts are beautiful, but the creatures of the desert are easily harmed. We must treat the plants and animals of the desert with care.

ON SHARING A BOOK

When you share a book with a child, you show that reading is important. To get the most out of the experience, read in a comfortable, quiet place. Turn off the television and limit other distractions, such as telephone calls. Be prepared to start slowly. Take turns reading parts of this book. Stop occasionally and discuss what you're reading. Talk about the photographs. If the child begins to lose interest, stop reading. When you pick up the book again, revisit the parts you have already read.

BE A VOCABULARY DETECTIVE

The word list on page 5 contains words that are important in understanding the topic of this book. Be word detectives and search for the words as you read the book together. Talk about what the words mean and how they are used in the sentence. Do any of these words have more than one meaning? You will find the words defined in a glossary on page 46.

WHAT ABOUT QUESTIONS?

Use questions to make sure the child understands the information in this book. Here are some suggestions:

> What did this paragraph tell us? What does this picture show? What is a food web? How do plants depend on animals? Where does energy in the desert come from? What do we call animals that eat both plants and animals? How can people help to protect desert plants and animals? What is your favourite part of the book? Why?

If the child has questions, don't hesitate to respond with questions of your own, such as What do *you* think? Why? What is it that you don't know? If the child can't remember certain facts, turn to the index.

INTRODUCING THE INDEX

The index helps readers find information without searching through the whole book. Turn to the index on page 48. Choose an entry such as *plants* and ask the child to use the index to find out how plants make their own food. Repeat with as many entries as you like. Ask the child to point out the differences between an index and a glossary. (The index helps readers find information, while the glossary tells readers what words mean.)

LEARN MORE ABOUT

DESERTS AND FOOD WEBS

BOOKS

Campbell, Andrew. *Who Eats Who in the Desert?* (Food Chains in Action) Franklin Watts Ltd, 2005.

Galko, Francine. *Desert Animals* (Animals in Their Habitats) Heinemann Library, 2003.

Haldane, Elizabeth. *Desert* Dorling Kindersley Publishers Ltd, 2006.

Pipe, Jim. *Deserts* (Extreme habitats) Ticktock Media Ltd, 2007.

Pyers, Greg. *Desert Explorer* (Habitat Explorer) Raintree, 2004.

Royston, Angela. *Deserts* (My World of Geography) Heinemann Library, 2005.

Spilsbury, Louise and Richard Spilsbury. *Desert Food Chains* (Food Webs) Heinemann Library, 2005.

Whitehouse, Patricia. *Hiding in a Desert* (Animal Camouflage) Heinemann Library, 2003.

WEBSITES

Biomes of the World: Desert
http://www.mbgnet.net/sets/desert
Emily and Roderick take visitors on a road trip through the desert.

CBBC Deserts
http://www.bbc.co.uk/nature/reallywild/features/desert_index.shtml
This website has lots of information about deserts around the world with links to facts and photos of desert plants and animals.

GLOSSARY

bacteria: tiny living things made of just one cell. Bacteria can be seen only under a microscope.

cactuses: desert plants that have thick skin and spines instead of leaves

carnivores: animals that eat meat

consumers: living things that eat other living things. Animals are consumers.

decay: to break down

decomposers: living things that feed on dead plants and animals and break them down into nutrients

environment: a place where a creature lives. An environment includes the air, soil, weather, plants and animals in a place.

food chain: the way energy moves from the sun to a plant, then to a plant eater, then to a meat eater and finally to a decomposer

food web: many food chains connected together. A food web shows how all living things in a place need one another for food.

herbivores: animals that eat plants

lichens: plant-like living things that are part algae and part fungi

mammals: animals that feed their babies milk and have hair on their bodies

nutrients: chemicals that living things need in order to grow

omnivores: animals that eat both plants and animals

photosynthesis: the way green plants use energy from sunlight to make their own food from carbon dioxide and water

producers: living things that make their own food. Plants are producers.

INDEX

First published in the United States of America in 2008.
Text copyright © 2008 by Lerner Publishing Group, Inc.